"Rao Garuda is a retirem[illegible] distills his years of experience and wisdom into one indispensable read. Don't attempt to navigate the pitfalls of retirement planning without it!"

—David McKnight, Financial Advisor and Author of *The Power of Zero*

"Reading this book is a Must! For anyone who is ambitious and wants to be inspired to greatness!!!!"

—Bill Lindsey MSFS, AEP, RFC, Lindsey Financial, Inc.

"Rao Garuda has spent years in the field. His book is your roadmap to success—don't leave it behind."

—Mark Matson, President, Matson Money

"Rao Garuda's book goes a long way toward making the unpredictable predictable. His approach takes the surprises out of your life by controlling the controllables. In addition, he shares with you his years of accumulated wisdom which will enable you to go from a life of success to a life of significance...a don't miss read!"

—Simon Singer, CFP, CAP, RFC, The Advisor Consulting Group

THE MEANING OF MONEY

THE MEANING OF MONEY

Creating Not Just Wealth on Your Balance Sheet but Significance in Your Life and Joy in Your Heart

Rao Garuda

For more information contact:
Associated Concepts Agency
Toll-free: 800-255-6086

ISBN Paperback: 978-1-939758-71-2
ISBN eBook: 978-1-939758-72-9

Printed in the United States of America
Book Design: Dotti Albertine

Be a coach, not a one-trick pony.
There's a place for all the products.

Contents

Introduction

WEALTH—the accumulation of success, its symbols, and the personal satisfaction of security and power. It can be earned, given, and taken away. One person may enjoy every luxury wealth can buy without having the treasure of personal fulfillment. Another person with immense personal fulfillment may be bereft of a penny. Which of these people is wealthier?

Today, I am a wealthy man. Through personal financial success as well as hardships, I accumulated the symbols of material security. But it was through philanthropy that I gained immeasurable personal fulfillment. When I realized that sharing my financial assets with the world on a grand scale compounded my personal satisfaction, I became wealthy.

Generosity and asset protection are not oil and water. With a little bit of careful planning, they blend easily and build exponentially. I'd like to share with you the joy of giving and seeing how your gift benefits others in very big ways, while simultaneously teaching you how to protect your assets.

Allow me to share my story with you in the first part of this book. Then, after you've seen firsthand that creating joy in your heart is possible, allow me to show you how to be ruler of your kingdom and benefactor to the greater good.

Chapter 1

My Road to Success, Significance, and Joy

WHEN I arrived in this country half a century ago, I had nothing but seven dollars in my pocket and a dream of making a difference. I'd been fortunate enough to receive a full scholarship to attend graduate school for structural engineering at the University of Colorado. My father, one of the hardest workers I've known, dropped me off at the airport in India for my flight to the United States. His parting words were simple: "I was only able to borrow enough money to buy a one-way ticket to the U.S.A., but don't worry—you are going to a country that offers the greatest opportunities for financial success. You will do very well. Good luck, and God bless you."

My father was a very intelligent, hardworking man. At the time that he purchased my plane ticket, he was providing financially for not only his six children but also four of his sisters, two brothers, and all of their children. His own father had been a wealthy shipping agent whose business was exporting goods to different countries and guaranteeing their safe delivery. Unfortunately, one of my grandfather's shipments was lost due to an accident, and his business went bankrupt. Corporate immunity hadn't yet been developed, and he had to sell all of his and my grandmother's assets to get by. My father, who was only eighteen, had to step in to help support the family. I was just six years old when I learned about my grandfather's bankruptcy and its consequences on the family's finances and lifestyle. It was at that early age that I first began to comprehend the value of asset protection and fiscal fitness—though I wouldn't know the exact terminology until many years later.

My father had graduated from high school with the highest honors, but he wasn't able to attend college because he had to work to support his family. He went on to self-educate himself, however, and eventually, he was able to start a business. No matter how much he earned, though, money was being consumed faster than it was being made because he had so many mouths to feed.

Even with his excessive financial burden, my father made sure that each and every one of his children—and later, his grandchildren—graduated from college. Many of his grandchildren, following the blueprint of my success, found their way to the United States for better careers and brighter futures. They all realized, as my father had, that the greatest gift a parent can give to his children is education. Knowledge can't ever be stolen.

In India, I'd gone to college for engineering. After receiving my father's generous gift of a one-way plane ticket, I attended graduate school as planned in Colorado, and then began my career with my first engineering job in Cleveland, Ohio. I returned to India briefly to get married, and once my wife and I were wed, we returned to Cleveland to settle down.

However, I had one problem with my engineering career: I wasn't quite making enough to support the income taxes I owed. In 1976, we found ourselves in the 70 percent tax bracket, and my wife, who was a physician, had to pay my income taxes. It was then that I began to realize that something needed to change. I knew I couldn't possibly be the only person struggling with huge tax obligations, so I decided to find a way to ease that strain.

I knew that the best possible way to change our situation was for me to take things into my own hands. Becoming a tax attorney seemed like it was the best option for me; it meant that I would learn how to cut my own taxes. I was advised to attend the two-year program at Ohio Paralegal Institute, and after receiving my associate degree from there, I would continue on to traditional law school. I finished the two-year program, and after graduation, I started taking courses in business school and began my career as a financial advisor. Several attorney friends of mine graciously helped me establish myself in the financial services business, and with their encouragement, I began to design large pension plans that significantly reduced income taxes, provided tax-free growth, and allowed clients to ultimately withdraw the funds on a tax-free basis.

After I graduated from the Ohio Paralegal Institute, I began to work for National Life Group and quickly became an independent advisor. The year I started, my income quite literally quintupled, and soon after that, I joined the top 1 percent "club." With time and experience, I was able to streamline my approach to advisory. I realized it was crucial to accomplish four things in order to maintain and grow wealth:

1. develop a consistent, predictable, guaranteed stream of income;
2. minimize income taxes;
3. minimize losses in the stock market; and
4. provide asset protection from lawsuits.

In 1978, I founded Associated Concepts Agency, Inc., and I also became a founding member of First Financial Resources, LLC. During this learning period, I acquired two financial services degrees from the American College in Bryn Mawr, Pennsylvania. I became a Chartered Financial Consultant and a Certified Life Underwriter. This process of lifetime learning still continues as of today; I strongly believe that the road to excellence is always under construction and that learning should never stop. To date, I continue to devote almost three months each year exclusively to bolstering my knowledge of my field in a continually evolving world. This indeed has become my passion: to learn as much as I can and use that knowledge to assist others.

One of the most important concepts at my company is that of putting our clients' minds at ease. I know what it's like to struggle to fall asleep at night, worrying about money. Watching my grandfather's company go bankrupt when I was just six years old taught me the value of asset protection and planning early on. I also know what it's like to lie awake, unhappy with life. My goal is to assist people with their wealth—minimizing their losses, yes, but also helping them to find the thing made possible by their wealth that brings them joy.

The shift in my focus from finding financial success to finding significance came about after I witnessed great difficulties and hardships, many experienced by those close to me. I will share just one of those stories with you, and I hope that you can relate to it in some way. I also hope it can inspire you to accept that tough times will come to you, and those around you, but in all instances, they will pass, and success will come after. As the Reverend Robert

H. Schuller once said, "Tough times never last, but tough people do."

About fifteen years ago, my wife and I found out that she had a heart problem. For a long time, we thought it was just a heart murmur—we didn't realize it could be bigger than that.

Finally, a friend of hers said, "Listen, you should really get this checked out." So we went to the Cleveland Clinic to see Dr. Cosgrove, who is one of the country's foremost heart surgeons and president of the Cleveland Clinic Foundation. After examining my wife, he told us that she was not yet ready for an operation, but that she probably would be in a couple of years. In the meantime, she would have to stop practicing medicine in order to ease the stress.

Ultimately, easing stress wasn't enough, and my wife had to undergo an aortic valve replacement. Thanks to Dr. Cosgrove and the power of modern medical technology, the operation was successful. The doctor told us that these procedures generally keep a patient healthy for ten years. It has now been fifteen years since my wife's surgery, and she is still in good health.

However, over the course of her illness, my wife

had been quite distressed—not only because she was very sick but also because she couldn't work. She didn't want the entire financial burden of our family to be on me. I was very grateful to be able to tell her that she didn't have to work. Our family had come a long way financially, and she didn't need to fret about our income. I was able to say to my wife not just "don't worry about finances," but something much more important: "I want you to enjoy life. You've paid your dues, and you should live your dream. So tell me what exactly your dream is. What would be your dream life?"

No one should underestimate the value of joy and satisfaction in their hearts. Speaking with my wife, it dawned on me that after a certain point, it is necessary to make the transition from success to significance. We had both experienced a great deal of turmoil, fear, and agony during her illness, not just from a financial perspective but from a perspective of satisfaction with life. As we struggled through this difficult time, we both began to see that we were on a life-long journey full of challenges and that we had to learn how to navigate that journey. I now understand that we are on this earth to make a difference—to enhance not only our own quality of life, but also that of others.

When I asked my wife, "What is your dream?" her response was, "I'd like to spend three or four months a year in Sai Baba's ashram in India." Sri Sathya Sai Baba was a guru and spiritual leader who I'd first been exposed to about twenty-five years earlier. He preached a simple, but powerful message above all else: to help ever, hurt never, and to love all, and serve all. My wife's dream was to learn more from him, and so together, we did just that. That year, I helped her to make the journey to India. Now, every October, she and I make the same trip. I stay for two weeks, and she stays for a few months, practicing meditation, spirituality, and service. In February, I return to India, and we make the trip home together.

Through Sai Baba's teachings and also through my own experience, I've learned that nothing brings joy to the heart like giving. I found great similarities between his teachings and the teachings of Jesus—and indeed, of most other faiths. A predominant principle in these teachings is that you cannot outgive God. My first large charitable donation was for $250,000, made in December of the year that my wife first decided to study in Sai Baba's ashram. I was certainly nervous about giving that much, but in the month of January, my income was $270,000. Your giving must be driven by unconditional love, but if you give from that genuine place, God gives back.

I've found my joy and satisfaction. I love what I do, and I love giving back to others. My wife is healthy and happy, and we have two wonderful sons—one even followed in my wife's footsteps and became a physician, and the other followed in mine and works in financial services. I am seventy-two years old, and I have no intention of stopping my work of love and service. I want to see a world that lives with the same kind of inner peace that I have, and I know I have the tools to help shape that world.

I had been blessed to have the privilege of giving away more than $1,000,000 of my own money thanks to Dan Sullivan, founder of a wonderful advisory company for entrepreneurs called Strategic Coach. I realized that I, too, could be instrumental in helping many professionals, business owners, and entrepreneurs—essentially, all those who make a huge difference in the economy and create multimillion-dollar foundations—realize their own joy and fulfillment. So I set myself a humble goal of saving up a minimum of $500 million to give to charities of all denominations. I, and all other advisors, have the tools, technology, and skills needed to assist our clients in accomplishing their goals and dreams. This process-driven technology—this unique ability—is what we are blessed with.

Finding Significance

A great number of people—including myself at times—measure their success by how much money they have accumulated to take care of their needs. Most of the financially successful people I interact with, however, are not completely satisfied or happy. It seems strange. If they're that wealthy, why aren't they happy?

The truth is, despite their great wealth, they haven't found significance in their life. There's something missing. There's a gap. The people who are able to cross that gap and really answer to themselves have achieved significance. That is the satisfaction and the happiness that makes life worth living: the knowledge that they've made a difference for others by contributing to their quality of life.

One of the founders of the Hard Rock Café, Isaac Tigrett, used some of his assets to build a huge hospital in Bangalore, India. It's a beautiful building, with extraordinary architecture and art, and it has a beautiful mission: to provide free health care for the poorest of the poor in nearby villages. Doctors, nurses, and other professionals from all over the world volunteer at this place. The first doctor that I met there was a heart surgeon from the Los Angeles General Hospital who worked at the Bangalore facility for six months out of the year. When I asked him why he chose to spend so much time at this hospital, he said to me, "I have enough money to buy anything in the world. But I don't have satisfaction and joy in my heart unless I'm giving, treating these people who are so poor that they don't have anything at all."

That's what you want in life: joy in your heart. And how do you create that joy? By helping people. There is no conflict between making money and helping people. If you have plenty to spare, why not put it toward something greater? Men like Warren

Buffet and Bill Gates give the majority of their income to charity. Money simply does not drive them anymore—their drive is their sincere desire to make a difference. I have yet to see more loving, giving, and compassionate people than Americans. Unfortunately, this is a well-kept secret.

I derive my joy from helping others find theirs. It took me a long time to get to this place, and there is certainly about twenty years' worth of my life that I spent making many mistakes and fixing them. You don't have to be a billionaire to be happy, but money is a convenient tool to do a lot of wonderful things and help a lot of people. Anyone can have that peace and satisfaction if they are willing to do a few things differently and have access to the right kind of advice and financial coaching.

When you walk with purpose, it becomes effortless, like breathing. You collide with destiny, for once you discover your purpose in life, your destiny is within sight. Some people work hard to make a living; I and others like me work hardest for those things we thrive on that money can't buy. We are beneficiaries of the past, trustees of the present, and architects of the future. Our goal should be not just to *inform* but to *transform*, by means of the power of love.

Planning Beyond Money

Many financial planners and other professionals that I know don't understand how they can make a difference—and they don't take that goal into account when planning. Most are focused on how to increase income. All of the conversations are about getting bigger returns on investments, making more money, creating better portfolios, and so on—and those conversations are meaningless without the support of a conversation on significance.

Therefore, I ask my clients the same thing I asked my wife after her diagnosis and surgery: If money were not an issue, can you describe how you would like to spend the rest of your life? When you can answer that question, I can help you begin on the path to significance.

There are two very important days in everyone's life. The first day is the day you're born. The second is the day you find out *why*. I have a list of twenty "must-answer" questions that I use to help my clients determine their path to significance. The very first one is: What's the true purpose of money? That is, what is that purpose that is more important than money itself?

This is a question that many people don't stop to ask themselves. When I bring it up with my clients, the conversation suddenly shifts. It's no longer about money management or investment, or how much money you have, or how I can make more money with your money. All of that becomes meaningless. Every single answer that my clients have given follows along a similar line: "I started with nothing. I wanted to achieve financial independence in my life—and I wanted to make a difference."

The question of purpose always leads to the next question: How, then, do we make a difference, or how do we enhance the quality of life? I find that deep down, everyone wants to be able to serve. I say that the true purpose of money is love. It's not how much money you have, it's how much of a difference you can make. Mahatma Gandhi once said, "My life is my message." In Sai Baba's teachings, that quote evolves into "My life is my message; your life is my message." Everyone has this concept embedded deeply inside them; it's just a question of bringing that practice into play. By focusing your life as your message, you can close the gap between "inform" and "transform."

There's Always a Way to Make a Difference

Significance is by no means limited to individuals with high net worth. There are three kinds of people: the first is the kind with money; the second is the kind with education, talent, and skill; and the third is the kind with time. All three of these assets can be used for the betterment of others. If you find you have a difficult time making significance happen with just your one asset, find other people with the complementary assets. You don't have to have the money. You don't have to have the talent. You don't have to have the time. If you can find other people with these assets who are like-minded and share the same spirit, you can achieve significance. If it's done with absolute unconditional love, if it is pure and selfless, then there is no limit to what you can accomplish.

A client of mine was able to go to Calcutta and spend some time following and learning from Mother Teresa. During his stay, Mother Teresa ventured into a very, very poor community, so dirty and filthy that many would not venture into it. There, Mother Teresa stumbled upon a man with leprosy dying in a gutter. She simply lifted him up with her bare hands and began to comfort him. My client watched in awe, and said to her, "Mother, in the Western world, where I come from, no one would do what you've just done, even for a million dollars." Mother Teresa responded, "In our mission, we do for God what we would not do for anyone else, even for a million dollars. And that is absolute unconditional love." This is what we need to practice.

Significance and purpose come to different people in different ways. In my case, it came to me in India, where I watched children learn in dilapidated one-room schoolhouses and saw people walk barefoot for two miles on dirt roads just to find drinking water.

I even recall a story a friend of mine told me about his time in India. Visiting northern India once, he knocked on the door of a house. A woman answered, saying, "There are two of us here, but the other woman can't come to the door." When my friend asked her why, she replied, "Well, we only have one set of clothes, and we share it every day." Now that's poverty. When you can give those women another set of clothing, that's significance. I cannot measure success by how much money I have, but I can certainly measure it with the joy in my heart when I help people.

When you do God's work, you become God in disguise. When I ask my clients, "What is your purpose? Who are you, really?" I then tell them that they're not who they think they are. They are an embodiment of divinity—God in disguise. So how, then, do you do His work? Through action, you transform work into worship and love.

There are always ways and means of realizing your dreams. As Vince Lombardi said, "The opposite of winning is not losing; it's quitting." If you were to die today, what dreams would die with you?

It's not enough just to focus on making a lot of money. I feel I would not be doing a complete job if I didn't focus on significance too. Success cannot be completely defined without significance. A successful life is one where you really have made a difference, and this is something I'm finding out through all of my clients, especially those of high net worth. These are people that have made it. They sacrificed an unbelievable amount and took huge risks, they made a lot of money, and now they want to make a difference. Yes, they "built it."

Do not falter if you find challenges along the way. I once ran into a multimillionaire who told me, "I like to live in the fast lane, but I hit a speed bump. I just took it as a message from the Good Lord." Great troubles and even tragedies can be great gifts as you aspire to achieve significance. Like the butterfly emerging from the cocoon, you must struggle, and in the end, you will crack the shell and emerge with strength. It is indeed the struggle that gives the butterfly's wings the strength to fly away. If you accept the challenge, you will become successful, and you will have had the opportunity to develop a healthy attitude of gratitude along the way.

The clients of mine who have achieved significance are now completely transformed from their former selves. They have jobs that they love in fields that they love, but they have moved above even that; now that they're contributing to the world, they're excited. Doctors, engineers, entrepreneurs, teachers—all of them come to me, saying, "Now I see that accumulating these assets specifically to make a difference is a worthwhile endeavor. Now I can see that what I need to do is give my children the best education possible and not just worry about leaving them a lot of money, because I have better ideas and better uses for my money." This is how to make a difference.

Chapter 2

The Joy of Giving (And How to Give to the Charities You Cherish, Encouraged by the IRS!)

WHEN I ask my clients whether they have any charitable habits, I often see an inner conflict as they find the answer. Most people have to be very convinced that they have enough money to sustain them, because if they give away money and then end up needing it, they won't be able to get it back. When I prepared to make my very first large charitable donation many years ago, I asked my wife and children what they thought. The first thing my wife said was "Do we have enough money?" It's a question that crosses everyone's mind as they prepare to donate. Do we have enough money? What *is* enough? Are we sure we can really part with it?

I have four brothers and a sister, and all of them were inclined to keep the money I wanted to donate in the family. "Why don't you give that money to us?" they asked. "Why would you give all that money to a charity?"

Donating a large amount of money is not an easy thing to do. You must have the utmost confidence that it's okay to part with your money. It is very different from giving small amounts—ten dollars, twenty dollars, or even one hundred dollars. To write a check for a large amount of money takes character and self-confidence. You cannot, however, achieve those things if you don't know why you're giving.

Voluntary Philanthropy

Early on in the advisory process, I ask my clients if there are any charitable causes that they support. With a great deal of hesitation, some of them say, "We're not really interested in any charities."

When I hear that response, I always look at their tax return, dumbfounded. "I don't understand this," I like to say. "You are very, very charitable."

"What do you mean?" they ask, confused. "What are you looking at?"

I tell them, "I'm looking at your 1040, and I can see right here that you paid five hundred thousand dollars to a charity named...the IRS."

They always laugh. In fact, we can change this practice of involuntary charity. I ask the right questions, find out what my clients care about or empathize with, and when we can figure out what's near and dear to their heart, we can start to talk about donating to real charities.

The truth is that you don't have to change your nature to become a charitable person. You simply have to change your plan. Everyone has an absolute expense that they rarely, if ever, exceed. Say you are currently paying one hundred thousand dollars in taxes every year. You can reduce that amount to fifty thousand if you take the time to understand charitable planning strategies.

You have the choice to become a philanthropist accidentally or voluntarily. Most people who do no planning become accidental philanthropists by giving a big donation to the IRS. But the IRS actually encourages people to give to charitable organizations. These groups do the job for which the federal government essentially has responsibility. When you voluntarily become a philanthropist and donate to tax-exempt charities (501c3s), your tax obligations will be significantly reduced. The government gives you a choice to become that charitable person. Would you prefer to serve, or would you prefer to send your money to Washington, D.C., on a one-way street?

When you give, you receive tenfold. What I can do is help you develop a zero-tax plan, which will give you the ability to experience the joy and satisfaction of helping others while you are still living and saving for yourself.

Minimize Your Taxes

On the list of my twenty "must-answer" questions for my clients is a standard question asked by most financial advisors: What is your biggest expense? I've heard a host of different responses—children, mortgage, utilities, wives, personal expenditures—but the answer for everyone, regardless of other expenses, is the same. Taxes are the single biggest expense for Americans.

To date, there are fifty-nine different taxes that we pay. Most people don't think about anything beyond income taxes or real estate taxes. However, there are taxes everywhere, on everything: your vehicles, your utilities, your pension plans. The taxes on pension plans are often the biggest of all.

The IRS and Your IRA

When my clients come to me and explain how much money they have in their IRA, I usually ask, "Whose money is it? Is it yours or theirs?"

My clients will always give me a puzzled look and say something in the vein of "I just said that this money is mine."

"No," I'll say, "it's theirs. How do you spell *theirs*? T-H-E...I-R-S. The IRS."

The money you have in an IRA is subject to an estate tax (also known as a death tax) and income tax. Suppose you have $1 million dollars in your IRA, and no other assets. You've arranged for your children to receive the money when you pass away. However, before they get a single penny of that inheritance, they must pay a federal income tax and a state income tax. There are also other taxes that we call "stealth taxes," because you don't perceive them to be increases—Medicare, Social Security, loss of itemized deductions, and more.

For our purposes, imagine you live in the state of California. With the federal income tax currently at 39.6 percent and the state of California income tax at 13.3 percent, your children will have to pay a total of 52 percent just on income tax. Before they pay the income tax, they will also have to pay an estate tax. That is roughly 50 percent, and then they will pay income tax on whatever is left over.

The biggest problem—besides, of course, the loss of most of the money—is that there must be other assets available to pay these taxes. If there aren't, then money must be withdrawn from that $1 million IRA account, *and that withdrawal will be taxed as well.* When you withdraw money from an IRA, there is always a tax on the withdrawal. If you withdraw $600,000 to pay the tax on $1 million, then you'll need to withdraw $300,000 to pay the tax on the $600,000, and so on. It becomes a tax on a tax on a tax, and it is a vicious cycle. Eventually, the balance in your IRA will be equal to the tax that must be paid.

A Roth IRA is a fantastic substitute for an IRA. There, the money grows tax-free, and you can withdraw the money tax-free. You must pay a small tax in the beginning, but the end result will yield more profit. If you were a farmer, would you rather pay a tax on the seeds or on the harvest? By combining Roth conversions with charitable planning, you can significantly reduce taxes and reap the benefits.

Tax-Free Investments

I recently took on a couple who make $300,000 a year. Their taxes amount to approximately $100,000. They'd told me they needed only $36,000 a year to maintain their lifestyle. They'd been seeing a CPA prior to coming to me, and at the end of every year, he did their tax return and then put the rest of the money into a CD.

"Do you know what CD stands for?" I asked the husband.

"Certificate of deposit."

"Wrong," I said. "It's a certificate of disappointment."

The reason for the disappointment in this particular investment is that a CD only pays minimal interest. Even on that minimal interest, which is usually less than 1 percent, you must pay taxes.

We have a number of tools to help your money

grow tax-free, and after we establish how much money you need for your lifestyle, we decide upon the appropriate tools for you. Municipal bonds are tax-free—although I recommend not investing in them if you live in a city that is not doing well—as is the aforementioned Roth IRA. There are other investment choices that I recommend because of their stability, such as income annuities and life insurance. Plans offered by many high-quality insurance companies guarantee that you will never lose money.

Avoidance Versus Evasion

Ralph Waldo Emerson wrote, "It requires a great deal of boldness and a great deal of caution to make a great fortune. And when you have got it, it requires ten times that much wit to keep it."

By considering how to pay your taxes appropriately, you can comfortably conserve and maintain a large percentage of your wealth. Recently, Mitt Romney has been subject to public complaints because he has only been paying 15 percent income tax. Romney has not done anything illegal at all; he has only taken advantage of tools and techniques hidden in the tax code. Above all, his great philanthropy was not recognized or admired appropriately.

There are currently more than 70,000 pages in the income tax code. The average American is not very familiar with what those pages contain. It is common practice for financial planners to talk about insurance, annuity, mutual funds, real estate trusts, and everything in between. They will talk about everything—except taxes. The majority of financial planners will not even mention taxes because they think that tax advice must come from a CPA or a tax attorney. However, CPAs don't typically solve the problem of how to cut their clients' taxes because there's no real incentive behind to do so. The result, then, is that you have multiple advisors, but none of them take the responsibility to help you solve the tax problem.

My strategy is, as always, to first allocate to you what you need to provide guaranteed income and maintain your lifestyle. The next step is to put away the rest of your money in a tax-deferred program of investments so that you can continue to accumulate money tax-free, and withdraw your money tax-free.

This combination—cut taxes, grow tax-free, withdraw tax-free—is crucial to your success, and you will find very few advisors who can effectively handle all three parts of this equation.

The challenge of cutting taxes is one that I had to face myself all those years ago when my wife had to pay my income tax. I've become uniquely qualified in learning about this subject and helping people with the same problem. I encourage my clients to ask, "How can I cut my taxes?" and to keep asking that question until they find something that satisfies them and brings their taxes to a very low point. If a multimillionaire like Mitt Romney can bring his taxes down to 15 percent, then he has a very good plan. My goal is do something similar for my clients. Remember: Do you want to pay taxes on the seeds or on the harvest? I want to cut your taxes at the seed level, and then I will completely eliminate your taxes when it is time to reap your harvest.

Set Your S.M.A.R.T. Goals

I tell my clients to simply be smart, and to be S.M.A.R.T.—**Specific, Measurable** or quantified, **Attainable**, **Ranked**, and **Time-Bound**—in their goals. By considering these different factors, you can make investments for yourself that will grow your wealth in a stable manner. Invest in ways that will not deplete your resources, and then you can plan for the time ahead. We have what is called "zero-tax planning," and basically, it declares clarity of purpose, mission, and vision. Why do you want to cut your taxes? What do you want to see happen with your money?

Giving for the Joy

Once you have cut down your taxes and have your own money back in your hands, instead of with the IRS, you can begin to plan how to use that money with significance. The majority of my clients have a high net worth; they have more than enough money to maintain a standard of living and meet all of their needs for the rest of their lives. All needs they've identified are taken care of—all hobbies, all obligations—and there's still money left over. The U.S. government encourages its people to give to charities in exchange for tax deductions, so I have my clients identify their favorite charities and go from there.

It's not enough to write a check, though. You can use your assets—both financial and intellectual—to make a difference. When I visited some of Sai Baba's hospitals in India, I was able to speak with some of the doctors there. One of them told me this moving story:

"Last month, we created a cataract surgery camp, and we worked with around seventy patients. One patient of mine in his thirties came to the camp with his family. We performed the cataract surgery for him, and throughout his surgery and recovery, he still took care of his family, despite being unable to see for a time. When I finally opened the bandage, we were both shaking like leaves, and I saw tears rolling down his cheeks. This noble man said to me, 'Sir, all of my life, I've believed that there is a God. I've prayed to God, but I had no idea that I would meet him in person today.'"

In considering when and how much to give, I think to myself that it's not really my money—I am simply being a good custodian of the money that has been given to me. We came into being with nothing, and we're going to go out with nothing. It's what we do as custodians in between that truly matters.

Helping Others, Helping Yourself

I get together with a group of about ten colleagues and friends every Sunday for prayer and other spiritual practices. We decided as a group to volunteer at a soup kitchen once a month, and that we would bring supplies for that day and contribute our time as well. The budget for each soup kitchen day was between three hundred and four hundred dollars.

Last week, the group mentioned that there was difficulty coming up with the four hundred dollars for each month's soup kitchen day. This information shocked me, because the group includes many financially successful individuals. I couldn't understand how this group full of doctors and lawyers could not collectively come up with a spare four hundred dollars every month.

I made a decision then and there. I said, "Let's maintain this project for as long as we want, money aside. When you don't have enough money for the monthly volunteer day, just call me and I'll write you a check for it, be it the full four hundred dollars or just a percentage of it." I did this because I knew that I could give them tax-deductible money from my foundation; but more importantly, when I go to our monthly soup kitchen day, I have even greater satisfaction from being able to make a difference.

I used to take my children to the soup kitchen with me, and almost every time they went, someone would ask them, "Why are you doing this?" My children always replied, "I'm doing this because I'm serving myself. I'm not doing it for you. I'm doing it for me." What's in it for you? The joy and satisfaction of giving.

Once you experience the joy of giving, you will be hard-pressed to find something better. You must first take the chance and see what it does to you personally—see how you are changed by the ability to do something for someone when there's no possible way that they can do it for themselves.

Recently, I was in line next to an older woman at the supermarket. She was short fifty or sixty cents, and she was digging through her purse, hoping to scrape together some change. I had the ability to give her that fifty or sixty cents, and the joy in her heart when I offered was unbelievable. She asked if I was sure I could spare the change. My answer? "Absolutely. Please allow me to do this." This was a tiny act of kindness, but it made a huge difference for someone else.

Small acts of kindness and charity are sometimes the biggest. I tell people that even if you cannot oblige, you can speak obligingly. You may not agree with someone, but you can disagree politely and respectfully. There is no need to argue to a point where they're upset.

All of these are acts of kindness, and that translates into the joy of giving. It does not cost you anything. Even the simple act of being friendly to a stranger makes a difference. If you smile at someone, there's always a reaction; they will smile back at you. Even a small gesture like that is an act of kindness. That is the joy of giving.

Kindness may be its own reward, but seeing how generosity benefits others can fill your heart, and knowing you can give grandly without losing in the process is only a question of risk management.

CHAPTER 3

Protecting Your Castle

I like to tell my clients that one of my assignments is to match big balance sheets with big hearts. Giving to charity has nothing to do with your charitable approach—I can show you how to not run out of money and also how to give a lot to charity while you're still alive. You can see your donations in action.

Warren Buffet's favorite thing to say is "Never lose money." Minimizing losses is really the most important thing that people can do to keep giving to the charitable causes they cherish while maintaining financial security in their own lives.

Dealing With Risk

In order to minimize losses, you have to learn how to deal with risk. There are three things you can do with risk. The first option is to avoid the risk, which is more or less impossible. You have to play the game. The second option is to ignore the risk. You cannot ignore the risk, and to do so would be foolish. The last option is to manage the risk. Once you've made money, keeping what you make is often the biggest challenge, and it's one that is frequently neglected. You've built a spectacular castle. How are you going to protect it?

There are myriad risks you can fall prey to today. In recent decades, America has become somewhat of a lawsuit-happy country. When one feels wronged, it's easy to call on the law for retribution, and people in high-profile, high-paying jobs are often the target, whether it's deserved or not. Don't forget to protect yourself. You have built a beautiful castle, but have you built a moat around it as well?

A physician I know from Cleveland retired about fifteen years ago. Two years before he did so, he delivered a baby. The mother was a drug addict, and she was in terrible shape, so the doctor decided to deliver the baby at Mount Sinai Hospital, which was the closest hospital in the area. The baby was born with severe disabilities because of the mother's drug usage.

Seventeen years later—fifteen years after he retired—the doctor's doorbell rang. He was being sued for not delivering the baby at the county hospital, which had a neonatal unit that might have been able to prevent the baby's disabilities. He chose Mount Sinai Hospital because it was an emergency, and he was trying to protect and save the life of the mother. It made no difference to the jury. The judgment was more than $40 million. He had no protection on his assets, and almost two decades after one honest mistake, he lost everything.

Physicians are so busy practicing medicine that they never take the time to protect themselves. Entrepreneurs and successful artists are often the same way. Lawsuits come in many forms, and it's important to protect yourself from all angles. Even divorces are a common and unexpected threat to assets. With almost 50 percent of American marriages ending in divorce, protecting your assets is an unfortunate but necessary step to take. As you make your way through life, be cognizant of the dangers to your castle. You must be able to keep what you make.

Entitlement risk, unfortunately, is not a risk that you can protect yourself against—but you can mentally prepare for it. The government is in the process of redistributing wealth, and that's what can break into your castle. **Inflation** is another one you can't control, and yet can prepare for. I believe inflation will come roaring back. Now, in 2014, it is temporarily at bay because the federal government is trying to artificially control it, but it will come back—and when it does, you can be armed. **Taxes**, as we discussed in the last chapter, are also a huge risk controlled by the government.

The Stock Market: A World of Risk

The **stock market** also provides a huge amount of risk. It can go down at precisely the wrong time, and you must have a plan to ensure you don't go broke from your investments. **Asset allocation** can be quite important in this planning. How are your investments diversified? Do you have all of your eggs in one basket? I strongly believe that the greatness of America is based on the free market. A portfolio should have at least 12,000 different holdings in stocks and bonds in forty-five different countries, so that you won't ever lose everything all at once. Define and diversify those investments.

If you tell a typical stockbroker that you want him to invest your money and yet guarantee that you'll never lose any, he will look at you like you're crazy. I'm here to tell you that you're not crazy. You can eliminate losses in your portfolio if you want to, and still make a decent amount of money, better even than bank CDs or anything else, to support yourself.

All my clients come in with a particular conditioning that results from seeing ads and newsreels about marketing and big firms. In my mind, the media is the biggest obstacle to overcome. People are driven by emotions, so there's a certain amount of training I have to do to get my clients to understand the best moves to make. I call it coaching. The time to take risk is not when the markets are high and the media is telling everyone how wonderful it is. You have to actively decide how much risk you can take for yourself.

Weighing Your Options

Most people are unaware of the terms **put option** and **call option**, but they are crucial when it comes to understanding and managing your stock portfolio. A **put option** is designed to protect your principle—it's essentially a small insurance policy. You purchase insurance for your car, your home, and your health, so why not insure your stocks and portfolios as well?

Say, for example, that you purchase one thousand shares in IBM for $10,000 total. You can tell your stockbroker to get you a put option on those one thousand shares, which will guarantee that even if the value of IBM drops, you will still get your $10,000 back. A **call option** is similar and provides more upside potential.

You must make sure that you clearly spell out your goals to your stockbroker or financial planner. There are tools that you and your advisor can use, but many people simply don't know what they are or understand how they work. Keep looking for financial planners that will go the extra mile for you.

Consider an **equity indexed annuity**. An equity indexed annuity is basically a fixed annuity that allows you to invest your money and let it grow on a tax-free basis. (Remember: Minimize losses everywhere!) You can invest in any index: the S&P 500, the Hang Seng (the Chinese index), or the EAFE (the European index). If you have an equity indexed annuity invested in indexes that do well, your asset value goes up—but if they don't do well, you won't lose any money. This is where the put option comes in.

A fixed annuity is your best bet, because it's more stable and "insured," but a variable can be good in some areas as well. The downside is that it's less stable, and in general, the cost of a variable annuity can be 3 to 4 percent a year—much more expensive than an indexed annuity's typical 1 to 2 percent rate.

Another investment tool to use is an **equity indexed life policy**. It's a form of life insurance, and the advantage to it is that it grows tax-free and can be withdrawn tax-free. It also tends to pay quite well. Pacific Life Insurance Company, for example, offers a call option that will pay you 1.4 times a potential market increase, but if the market drops, you won't lose any money. Any of the above tools are useful to minimize your stock losses, particularly if you are preparing for retirement.

Risky Business

Psychologist Daniel Kahneman, a professor at Princeton University, won the 2002 Nobel Prize for his work in economics. He's very famous for saying that the stock market isn't about economics—it's about *psychonomics*. He essentially attributes losses in the stock market to human behavior.

We all know logically that we should be buying low and selling high to make money. Unfortunately, many people do the exact opposite. They save their money in a CD, earning less than 1 percent interest, and wait until the stock market goes up dramatically before they decide to invest. When the market crashes, everyone panics and wants to get out, so they sell everything at low value.

We use a technique called **rebalancing your portfolio**, where you take some of the profits from stocks that have gone up and reinvest the profits back into those that are underpriced. If you do that, you'll be forced to buy low and sell high, and it's a great technique to use to ensure that you're headed in the right direction. This process must be built in to accomplish the results automatically.

The next step to avoid risk is to invest in the

aforementioned equity index annuities. You've made money with your portfolio, and now you must protect your profits. When you invest those profits in your equity indexes, you'll never lose that money again, regardless of whether the value increases. Always remember that it's not just important to make money—it's important to keep it, too. Keeping what you make is the biggest challenge in the country right now, and it's a challenge that everyone faces.

The question you must always ask yourself is "How much risk can I take?" I ask my clients who are planning for retirement this question, and they all give me the same answer: "None of it." Yet they are 100 percent in the stock market—and that puts them at 100 percent risk. Make sure you've got harmony between your thoughts, words, and deeds. People have very good thoughts about not losing money, but they don't know how to do it. They don't take the steps to ensure that they have a plan, and in the long run, that is what takes them down.

Three Big Mistakes

There are three crucial mistakes that I see people make in their financial planning. The first is with regard to stock picking, the second is to timing, and the third is to track record investing. We want to be sure that people don't make these mistakes.

The concept of **stock picking** is quite common: If you know which stocks to pick, you'll become very successful. However, no one has been able to predict which stocks will perform, and which ones won't. Currently, there are more than 14,000 stocks available and 28,000 mutual funds. The purpose of a mutual fund manager is to pick the right stocks and show you how to make a lot of money—but if someone can do that, then why is it necessary to have 28,000 mutual funds? You need only one.

When you have that many mutual funds, word gets around about which ones are the most successful. Everyone will want to put their money in the successful few—but because of this, the funds that are successful this year will probably lose a lot of money next year.

This is **track record investing**: People invest in the stocks that have a good track record. Fidelity Magellan was a very popular mutual fund for a long time, as it had a track record of 15 percent annual return for fifteen years. The average Fidelity investors, however, lost money, because they got in and then got out at the wrong times.

Investors panic. It's a symptom of excessive media hype: When it becomes known that something is going wrong, everyone bails out. When something skyrockets, everyone buys. It's the emotional roller coaster, and that's where incorrect **timing** comes in. You cannot time the market. You can't predict when the market will go up or down any more than you can predict which stock will be successful. The key is to be passively invested, rather than actively invested (buying and selling constantly). If you have staying power and you can define what risk you can afford, then you can allow the market to work in your favor. Buy safely if that's what you need to do, and use tools to "insure" your money. Some people don't need to access the money they've invested for a few decades, so they can afford to be more aggressively growth-oriented in choosing their stocks. That's okay as long as they are prepared for their investment to drop *and* bounce back. Others are only interested in letting their portfolio fluctuate by 10 or 20 percent, and that's okay too, as long as you know your limits.

We believe that it is also crucial to have a well-diversified portfolio, meaning you have at least 12,000 holdings in many different countries. Diversity is what will help you maintain your stability—if there is risk in one area, another area will undoubtedly be more stable. With an **exchange-traded fund**, or ETF, you are able to have a basket of thousands of different stocks in different countries, and that will help you make money in the long run.

I often ask my clients if they're a thermometer, or a thermostat. A thermometer is reactive; the temperature does what it wants and the thermometer changes according to the temperature. A thermostat, however, is proactive. It sets the temperature and the precedent. You must become a thermostat, not a thermometer, to be successful in life. If you're a thermostat, the rules of engagement are clearly defined.

You've been conditioned to think about making money in the market through stock picking, through market timing, and through choosing the best-performing fund. None of those things will consistently help you. Since they won't, what you should be focused on is how to minimize your losses. Once you can do that, then you can put a certain amount of your money at risk and see what happens—but know that it truly is a gamble to put money into the stock market.

You can avoid the risk. You can eliminate the risk. You can transfer the risk. Or, you can choose to manage the risk. Once you've defined your cost of living, secured your lifestyle, and found ways to give back to the community, consider how to continue to make money off what you already have. We'll give you a portfolio that is designed to perform within the appropriate range, but also give you a return so that your wealth can continue to grow. There are many available solutions, but none of those solutions begins with risking your entire net worth on the market. Minimize your losses, and your wealth will last you a lifetime.

Build Your Team

The first step to protecting your wealth is to fully realize that you must do something. Find specialists who can help you—accountants, attorneys, financial planners, stockbrokers—anyone who knows the business and can be on your team.

When building your team, be aware of the fact that most of the financial planners who are strictly involved in stocks and trading only get paid when you buy stock. They get paid again when you sell it—so they have no real incentive to help you in a genuine way. My company offers a performance-oriented fee structure contract, which means that we do not get paid unless our clients make money. If they lose money, we get nothing. That way, we have an incentive to perform well. This practice separates serious planners from those who don't really know how to plan to the client's advantage. You must look for people that will work for you rather than work for themselves.

I call this a **results-oriented economy**. There are two kinds of economies in the world: the results-oriented economy, and the **time and effort economy**—in other words, "If you keep your money with me for one year, I'll charge you money, regardless of the results." Almost everyone is happy with a time and effort economy, or it just doesn't occur to them that we would all be better off with the results-oriented one. Entrepreneurs that are enormously successful get paid for producing results. That's what we want our clients to focus on.

I'm aware that this often sounds too good to be true. I tell people I can save them $200,000 in taxes if they pay me $20,000. It's not too good to be true. I'm a firm believer in process, having been trained as an engineer, and I'm aware that with media hype and uncommitted planners dominating society's impression of finances, process and education are not involved enough. Do your homework. Your advisor will help you, but you have to know for yourself what works and what doesn't work in order to stay on top.

Learn the Rules

The second point in protecting your wealth is to see exactly what the statutes are in the state where you live. Some states are very good in terms of helping you protect yourself. Texas and Florida protect all assets in an annuity or a life insurance policy, but that is not the case in California, or New York, or New Jersey. Some states do have protection, but they might limit it to $10,000 or $25,000.

Nevada has a very good asset protection statute. If you open an annuity or a life insurance policy, it is essentially protected after two years. Delaware, Alaska, South Dakota, Wyoming, and Oklahoma also have similar statutes. These statutes change all the time, though, so you must make sure that you get competent legal advice to help you.

Ownership and Control

The third point in protecting your wealth is jurisdiction. Where do you set up these asset protection trusts? Does it have to be onshore or offshore? Luckily, many states in the U.S. are very friendly. Ultimately, there are two words that are important in asset protection. One is **ownership**. The other is **control.** If you can give up ownership of an asset but retain control entirely (which means you'll have the ability to invest it anywhere and use it for anything that you need, but you do not own it), that's the ultimate form of protection. If someone wants to sue you but you don't own property, they can't take it away from you. Many people have difficulty giving up ownership, and if you're one of those people, find a state that will help you protect your assets.

If the Cleveland physician I mentioned earlier had set up a trust in Nevada, for example, then after two years, that asset would have been untouchable.

The charging order that he received in Ohio could not be levied against that asset in Nevada. He could have helped himself completely and protected his family if he'd done something like this. Kenneth Lay of Enron held annuities and a house in Florida. When Enron declared bankruptcy and he had large judgments in Texas, all of his money was protected.

IRAs are also protected by law, so if you have assets in an IRA, they'll be safe. If you're still working, the money in your pension plan is also protected—even large amounts. We have products now that not only guarantee your paycheck but also index your paycheck to inflation (up to 10 percent per year). Products like these are a great way to minimize your risk.

Pension plans also have protection from the Employee Retirement Income Security Act. ERISA is by statute. If you have money in a pension plan and you have a case with one or more employees, the money inside the pension plan is safe from lawsuits, even in the event of bankruptcy.

I had a client with $2 million in her pension plans. She was a real-estate agent, and she bought a large amount of real estate. However, the prices dropped when the market crashed, and the bank told her she had to put down more collateral or they'd foreclose on the property. She was worried, but because the majority of her money was in a pension plan, she wouldn't have lost much even if the bank did foreclose on her property.

If you can find the right specialists to guide you, you'll have many options to protect yourself. Do not hesitate to seek protection. You've spent your life building up your assets—why let them get away from you? Build your moat. Protect your castle. Then, from that place of security, you can focus on finding your path to significance. And what better time to find the true significance in your life than during a comfortable and secure retirement?

Chapter 4

Retire With Security, Significance, and Joy

OF all the journeys, I think the longest one is from the head to the heart. Whether people have $1 million, $5 million, $20 million, or $20 billion, their mind tells them that they don't have enough money—even when their heart is saying, "Let's give some of this away. This cause needs it." A client of mine has $20 million on hand from a lifetime of success as a dental surgeon. He's eighty-two, and he's still working.

"Why are you still working?" I asked when I first met him.

He responded quietly, "I'm not sure if I have enough money."

He and I sat down together, listed all of his expenses, and figured out how much money he needed to maintain a comfortable lifestyle. I then doubled the amount to make sure he had enough cushion to take care of himself in the event of an emergency.

His total need came to $5 million. He had $15 million of extra money.

When I explained this to him, he still was worried that he didn't have enough money. I took it to the next level.

"One of these days, you and your wife are going to pass away. What would you want that $20 million to go to?"

"I never thought about that," he said.

My next question was simple: "What's near and dear to your heart? What do you love?"

"Well," he said without needing any time to think about it, "I love my dental school. I love education. I want to make sure students don't drop out of high school, that they follow through in college—what if I give money for some scholarships?" The surgeon went on and on, inspired.

When I ask my clients what's close to their heart, they almost always tell me how they started with nothing. They wish that early on, someone might have helped them with scholarships, or guided them, or counseled them as they proceeded with their career. Identify what is close to you. It is easy to be compassionate when you truly understand a particular struggle.

My company follows a principle called "serve and deserve." What do we all deserve? God's grace, and joy and satisfaction in our hearts. When we serve—when we donate our time, our efforts, our money—we get what we need. We can reduce our taxes. We can increase benefits for ourselves and our families. We give, and we get joy. We get satisfaction.

The Risks of Retirement

There are twelve major risks you may face in retirement, some of which were discussed in the last chapter, and some of which we'll discuss below:

- Longevity Risk
- Entitlement Risk
- Excess Withdrawal Risk
- Market Risk
- Lifestyle Risk
- Asset Allocation Risk
- Sequence of Returns Risk
- Inflation Risk
- Medical Expense Risk
- Tax Risk
- Personal or Event Risk
- Incapacity Risk

One of the biggest risks people face today is **longevity**: What if you live too long and run out of money? In a recent seminar, I mentioned that my company is in the business of taking care of those that live too long or die too soon.

One elderly gentleman raised his hand. "What if I'm not lucky enough to die?" he asked me.

"What do you mean, 'lucky enough to die?'" I asked, confused.

"Well, the problem in America is living too long," he told me. "It's possible that I could live for a very long time, and what then?"

It's odd to think that living in itself is a risk, but if you don't plan accordingly, you could run into financial trouble simply by trying to live. In the years leading up to retirement, you need to be aware of **sequence of returns**, a risk that most people do not have covered. The most critical time period for retirement is five years before you retire and five years after, because if you lose money during that time, you can never recover it. Time your investments and your spending well, because you will need it.

In April 2013, *National Geographic* published an article that stated that humans could soon live to an average age of one hundred and twenty years old. A friend and I were joking about it, and he said to me, "Imagine this scenario: You're one hundred and twenty, and you're still in good health. You have to take care of your parents, who are both one hundred and forty years old. Unfortunately, your children, who are one hundred years old, have lost their jobs, and they decide to move back in with you. Is it possible?"

Not only is it possible, it's probable. With advances in medical technology, we are eradicating diseases constantly—one day, we may even eliminate some at conception itself. What if you do live until you're one hundred and twenty but you've only really planned to live until you're eighty?

Longevity also poses a **lifestyle** risk—what if your children and your parents *do* move in with you years after you've retired? Changes like this happen unexpectedly and often uncontrollably. You could also incur **incapacity** or **medical expense risk**. If you are diagnosed with any disease, from Alzheimer's to cancer, you'll have to pay for your care. That could drain a huge amount of money, especially with the cost of medical care rising indefinitely.

I had a very successful client who was an executive with a Fortune 500 corporation. He was a big, heavy man, built like a tank. We were in a group together that would meet once a week to talk about spirituality and philosophy. One day, when he was in his forties, he came to me and said, "I'm an MBA, and I know about finances. I know I need somebody I trust to take care of me and my finances—and I trust you. Will you do it?"

"Okay, no problem," I said. "I'll do it." I set him up with various investments and basic life insurance. "However," I told him, "this life insurance does not cover long-term care and nursing home care."

"I'm in great shape," he said. "Just look at me!" And it was true—although he was a big man, almost 250 pounds, he was in excellent physical shape.

Then, at age fifty-one, he was diagnosed with Parkinson's. It was already in an advanced stage, and his health deteriorated quickly. It wasn't too long before his very petite wife, who weighed maybe 100 pounds, had to change his diapers. She had no choice but to get help to care for him—care that ended up costing $10,000 every month. They had about $700,000 in savings, but it couldn't last forever. The only other money they had was $1 million in an IRA. So they pulled that out, paid the tax, and used the balance for the nursing home care.

After four years, his wife came to me. "Rao, if he lives two or three more years," she said, "we will be completely broke. We'll have to sell the house." Their accounts were completely drained, and there was nothing either of them could do to remedy the situation.

As it happened, he passed away a couple months after that conversation. His wife, who was an author and a poet, had to go back to work. If he had lived longer, they would have had to sell everything they owned and gone on welfare.

All of this could have been avoided if they had used financial products available now that include not only life insurance but also what I term "living insurance" or "living benefits." Living benefits enable you to prepay up to 95% of the death benefit included in life insurance to take care of home health care, nursing home care, or clinical care if you are diagnosed with a critical illness. Living benefits mean that you and your family will not go broke if you are faced with a critical illness.

Additionally, there are precautions you can take to protect your money even if you do need to make big payments for medical care. For example, you can insure your IRA. We insure our homes, we insure our businesses, we insure our health, but we don't think to insure our IRA. If you need home health care, if you have a heart attack or a stroke, you could easily deplete your IRA. However, if you have the right kind of financial products, you don't need to do that. Your IRA will be protected.

Review Your Policy Annually

A lot of older life insurance policies don't have the new features that will take care of you as you get age. A recent study conducted at MIT shows that three out of four couples over age sixty-five will experience one of the following issues: Alzheimer's, dementia, or Parkinson's. Most people don't have coverage for these diseases, and so illness is a common issue when it comes to risk and depleting resources.

Some of the newer polices include caveats to assist you later in your life. They define certain activities of daily living (ADL), and if you can't perform a certain number of the ADLs, then you will actually qualify to collect your benefits from your life insurance for home health care.

I recommend that you review your policies annually and make sure that each one has something to meet your needs. Holding on to an old policy without these newer features is like buying an old car without air bags or seatbelts. There are many advisors who will offer you a consultation or a second opinion at no cost or obligation, so don't hesitate to explore other options.

Creating an Exit Strategy—With a Guaranteed, Permanent Paycheck

Your **withdrawal** strategy is the final risk. How much is safe to withdraw from your retirement fund so that you never run out of money in your lifetime? The *Wall Street Journal* says 2 percent a year is safe. You must be diligent and careful, though, and avoid withdrawing excessively. If you have $1 million in the bank, and you take out 3 percent a year, that's $30,000 for the whole year—$2,500 per month. That may not even cover your rent or mortgage payments. That's why what you really need is a guaranteed, permanent paycheck.

A "guaranteed, permanent paycheck" sounds like it might be too good to be true—but it's possible, legal, and even common. The phrase defines what most know as a single premium immediate annuity (SPIA). You give money to the right insurance company, and in return, it pays you year after year.

When you sign up for an SPIA, the insurance company will have two questions for you. The first is "What do you want this money to do while you're living?" The other question is "What do you want this money to do when you die?" These are the very important questions that you must ask yourself, with or without an annuity.

A client came to me with $1 million in savings. "Rao," he said, "I'm seventy-five years old, and so is my wife. We don't have children. If I put my $1 million in the bank, I'll be lucky if I get $10,000 of income. That simply will not cut it.

"If I put the money in the stock market, I'll lose it, and that doesn't cut it.

"If I tie it up for a long time, I might be able to get 3 percent—$30,000 a year—no matter how long my wife and I live. That $30,000 is subject to income taxes, and it isn't indexed to inflation. That simply will not cut it.

"So," he finished, "what can you do for me?"

"Well," I said, "if you're not concerned about anything else except receiving the highest possible income as long as you and your wife live, we have a company that will give you $75,000 a year—90 percent of which is tax-free for the first ten years."

He stared at me. "Let me get this straight," my client said. "I get $75,000 a year, plus another $40,000 and change from Social Security, and I'm lucky if I get $10,000 for the whole year from the bank. Who does this?"

These are the SPIAs, and they are offered only by insurance companies. The stock market cannot do it for you. The bond market cannot do it for you. No one can do it for you except a life insurance company, and that is what is called a guaranteed paycheck for the rest of your life, in the form of an immediate annuity.

A different client came to me. "Rao," she said, "I want to make sure that I not only get my money but also health care coverage for my husband and me as well. What can you do for me?"

"There are some companies that will give you nursing home coverage in addition to SPIAs," I told her.

"Well," she said, "what if we're not so sick that we

have to go to a nursing home, but sick enough that we need someone to come to our home for help?"

She had a valid point. Some companies will give you $65,000 instead of $75,000, but if you need home health care, that $65,000 paycheck will turn into a yearly $130,000 to cover your home health care for five years.

A third client came to me. "I want income to continue for my children after I'm gone. And, by the way, is it possible for my grandchildren to receive that income too?"

"Yes, it is," I told him. "If you want income as long as you live, plus as long as your son lives, plus as long as your grandson lives, we can do that. The income will drop to $45,000, and it will last."

There are many different forms of this income, and none of them involve the stock market. A stockbroker might tell you that you could make more money investing in the stock market, but does the stock market guarantee that you'll never lose any money? Does the stock market guarantee a paycheck no matter how long you live—or how long your *grand*children live? The stock market does not. It requires risk that, in retirement, you might not be able to take. To maintain your accounts, you must keep eliminating risk.

There are so many different types of annuities that you must make sure you have the one that is right for you. Make sure you spell out your goals very clearly. What do you want? Do you want guaranteed income for yourself? For your wife? For your children? What about liquidity? Are there any surrender charges? What happens if you cancel your policy? Become knowledgeable before you jump in, and that will protect you as you move forward.

I recommend investing as much as you need to cover your fixed expenses in an SPIA. If you need $6,000 a month, then you invest $6,000, and the remainder of your income can be invested anywhere else. You can cover your monthly expenses with your return from these investments, and you won't have to panic if the market goes down.

Other Types of Annuities

Annuities used to have a very bad reputation because they didn't have much variety. Now, in 2013, there are several wonderful variations, and you can find the right annuity to suit your needs. There are options to take care of critical illness, options that provide death benefits, and options that provide long-term care. **Variable annuities**, as opposed to the fixed annuities described above, allow you to invest your money in the stock market in a sub-account. Normally, these annuities are more expensive, but they can still provide you with your guaranteed paycheck. They also have a convenient death benefit that pays if the markets go down or behave irrationally, so there's security in this choice as well.

Another option is an **indexed life insurance policy**. The indexed policy is invested inside a life insurance policy, and when withdrawn, it is tax-free. If you design and build the account properly, you can have your paycheck for life as well, with an added death benefit.

Many financial planners strictly like to buy and sell stocks, because they receive commissions for them. You must be careful about what specialists you use. I recommend that clients always ask their advisors, "Would you mind sharing with me your plan for yourself?" Find out what their plan is and if they have any money in the products that they recommend for you. If they're not operating in your best interests, they'll walk away from that question. You can use it to protect yourself.

Annuities may sound too good to be true, but in all honesty, they are too good *not* to be true. If you educate yourself and have specialists who understand the product, you'll pay and protect yourself for a lifetime.

An IDEAL Plan

As you embark on your planning journey, remember the acronym IDEAL, which I believe to be the most efficient plan:

Income planning, insuring your risks, and tax planning
Diversification of products and strategies
Equities are the best way to accumulate capital
Asset allocation and protection
Leverage

Leverage is a term that is used very commonly in the technical field; I like to call it "financial engineering." If money is used to acquire a properly designed life insurance policy, for example, then every dollar spent for this purpose will work as though it is several dollars. That is to say, the dollar is being spent specifically on a life insurance policy—but it will also solve the problems of living too long, dying too soon, critical illnesses, and so on. In all of these cases, that one dollar readily creates immediate cash when it is needed most, providing liquidity as well as "tax-free" funds. This is what leverage is all about—using one dollar and making it work toward several goals. Considering the concept of leverage in your planning is the last crucial step to making your IDEAL financial plan effective.

Unfortunately, in the financial planning business, there are many people who prescribe the solution before they diagnose the problem, because they only know one product. In medicine, as well as in financial planning, a prescription without a diagnosis is malpractice.

If you go to a doctor at any reputable hospital, he or she will first complete your history and check your physicals. A doctor won't just give you a prescription and say, "Go home and take these pills," before answering any questions. He or she will do a thorough checkup first, with blood tests and screenings and history, and then prescribe. It's the same with financial planning. Make sure you work with someone who asks questions, who is thorough, who starts with the strong foundation.

When I was an engineer, the first thing I would do in designing a building was to build a very strong foundation. The basement, built right on top of the foundation, is the safest place to stay during a tornado. No matter what happens, that foundation has to be strong enough to withstand the tornado.

Financial planning is not so different, and the foundation of financial planning is annuity and life insurance. Annuities are the strongest foundation, a guaranteed paycheck for life, and once you've put some money into them, you can build on top of them with other instruments, like the stock market. You should not, however, be investing before you save, or before you have a strong foundation. There's nothing wrong with investing in the stock market, and there's nothing wrong with annuities. But in order to have a strong castle, you must have it all: the foundation first, and the elaborate beauty later.

The Joy of Giving in Retirement

When you have a guaranteed, permanent paycheck, when you don't have to worry about your financial security in your old age, and when you don't have to stress about going broke if you are diagnosed with a critical illness, you can truly commit to finding significance in your retirement.

Roughly thirty years ago, I met an older man named James Johnson in a bank. He approached me, seeing that I was Indian, and he asked me if I knew the teachings of Sai Baba. We quickly found that we had in common a deep admiration for Sai Baba, and we started to get to know each other.

As we became friends, James revealed more about himself to me. "I'm a retired engineer," he said, "and I don't have a lot of money, but I do get Social Security." He went on to tell me that he felt he only needed about half of the Social Security money that he was receiving. I told him that it was great that he was saving, and we kept talking. We talked about generosity, about religion, about philosophy.

One day, James came to me, asking for a favor. "My sister passed away recently, and she left me a lot of money," he said. "But I don't need it. My financial advisor told me to put the money in a trust, so I did—but I'm done with it. I want to give that money to charity, and my advisor won't let me do it."

"Why not?" I asked.

"He told me that I might need the money for myself one day, and that he had a fiduciary obligation to ensure that my money was saved for that future possibility. I don't want to save it. I would rather give it to some charities—maybe a hospital so that they can provide free services, or to collect drinking water for people who don't have it."

"Okay," I said. "What would you like me to do?"

"I'd like to fire him. And I'd like for you to take all that money and give it away."

"James," I said, "I can't do that. Your advisor is right—what if you need the money? What if you need to pay a nursing home or hospital expenses?"

James thought about it. "Well, can you give me ideas on how to donate only some of the money?"

I agreed to crunch some numbers and see what I could do. "I'm pretty sure you can give away about half of the money, since you're not even using all of your Social Security for your lifestyle."

"Perfect—but there's one condition," said James.

"What's that?"

James looked me in the eye and said, "I don't want anybody to make an announcement that I gave the money to the organization. I want to do this anonymously."

"Why?"

"Well, see, it's an ego trip. I don't want or need to feel proud that I did this. It's not my money. It's God's money, and it should go back to Him. I just want to be a good trustee of that money."

I respected that thought, and James and I made it work. We agreed that when he passed away, he would leave more of the money to a charity of his choice.

Later on, when James was in his nineties, he asked me to help him pick out a nursing home. I made some appointments, took him for visits, and he chose one. "In two weeks, Rao," he said, "you go ahead and put me in there. You have enough money to take care of me." I agreed, and he began to make arrangements and pack up his home. A week before I was supposed to help move him into the nursing home, he passed away peacefully in his sleep.

James was an inspiration and a blessing. "A lot of people have desires," he would always say to me, "but you have to have a limit on those desires. Man minus desires equals God. That's the only difference."

What James knew about generosity is what so many of us struggle with when we arrange our wills—what will be the impact of a generous inheritance on those we love?

Chapter 5

Leaving a Legacy of Significance and Joy

MANY of my high-net-worth clients tell me they struggle when they draw up their wills. They hesitate to leave too much money to their family, lest they spoil the next generation. This is one of the ongoing conflicts in American society today—should we provide financial assistance, and if we do, then will the recipients become less inclined to work? Unemployment benefits, for example, have gone from a six-month term to a two-year term, and it is still up for debate as to whether to increase them again. Where, though, is the incentive to work if the government will provide money for years? We talk about civil rights, but not about civil responsibilities.

Rights and responsibilities are two arms on the body of society. They must work together; they cannot operate by themselves. When you give, you also create some responsibility. You create accountability. In general, charities tend to be more efficient in spending their money than the federal government. Many of my clients are hesitant, and initially feel that there's too much risk, too much abuse, and too little accountability to donate. However, the only way to truly control the destination of your money is to donate yourself.

In death, taxes will still come out of your savings. One of the benefits of making room in your current plan for charitable donations is that you can avoid those taxes as well. I met with a client recently who thought he wasn't inclined to give at all. When he realized that he would have to pay taxes even after he and his wife passed away, he started to think differently about charities. We identified causes that were close to his heart—he was a strict vegetarian because he did not like violence toward animals—and suddenly he realized that he could contentedly leave money to animal shelters, knowing that in death, his donations would support something he strongly stood for in life.

Leaving a Legacy

A great way to leave a lasting legacy is to set up a family foundation. Your children, grandchildren, and great-grandchildren can become trustees of that foundation, and that job will enable them to see exactly how their contribution transforms society. Creating a foundation ensures that you are instilling generous values in your children, and you can also make sure that your wealth does not spoil your children's mentality.

People who have not seen true poverty often have the expectation that if they want something, at some point they're going to get it without having to do much work. Familial wealth can breed a certain amount of unhealthy entitlement. As you create generosity in yourself, find a way to create gratitude in your children so that they may carry your message of love and pass it on.

I used to take my children to places of poverty, simply to demonstrate that they should be grateful and see what the alternative to their wealth could be. I'd say, "Kids, this is what could happen if you don't study hard, and if you waste or misuse your money. But if you're willing to give up something that you really want, and use that money to buy these other kids clothing, would you like to do that?" These trips scared the daylights out of my children but also encouraged them to work hard and give with purpose.

The key is exposure. Children have to see what you have provided for them. They have to see how the rest of the world lives. If you're too busy and don't give them that exposure, then they never even have a chance to appreciate what you do or how you do it. You have to get them involved. My family goes downtown every other week. We work in shelters for battered women. We go to soup kitchens. We go to the poorest of the poor places, and our children serve food to these people or give them clothing. You have to engage your children in this conversation, because otherwise they won't see what poverty truly means and why it's up to them to make a difference.

Plan Before You Go

A twenty-year study indicates that 70 percent of estates fail to transfer wealth successfully to the next generation. Of the 30 percent of estates that do transfer, 70 percent of those fail to pass on to the generation that follows. The result is that 90 percent of estates vanish by the time they've reached the third generation. The cost is devastating: It is not only the loss of financial inheritance, but also the loss of a legacy, which could in turn lead to the breakdown of a family.

A classic case of failed transfer is Joe Robbie, the original owner of the Miami Dolphins. Upon his death, he was worth approximately $400 million, but his children got next to nothing because he did not plan accordingly. There was no money to pay the excessive estate tax on the $400 million that was left to them. Ultimately, in order to pay the tax, the family was forced to sell the assets, including the Miami Dolphins and the stadium named after Robbie, and there was no legacy left. What might it cost you, your spouse, your heirs, and your legacy if you don't get your planning right before you're gone?

Consider how much you'll need to provide for your loved ones, and then create an opportunity to make it happen—instead of creating a situation like that of Joe Robbie and so many others. You can effectively leave your money behind for your heirs in a life insurance policy. If you wish to leave $1 million for your heirs in your life insurance policy, you'll need to pay annual premiums of anywhere from $10,000 to $30,000. Your legacy will be successfully transferred, and you will have only paid 1 to 3 percent on it each year. You're making an investment while you still have control. If you don't, your loved ones are required to do it later, and they probably will not know how to do it. Be able to preserve your hard-earned estate.

Turn your financial planning into an opportunity to achieve your objectives while you can still experience the joy. A key way to minimize your estate tax is to donate now. You will be able to give more. You can see your donation in action right now—which is always when it is most needed. You can rest with peace, knowing you've done all you can with your wealth. Most importantly, you can plan from your heart and enjoy the fruit of your labor today.

My father mentioned a family foundation in his estate document when he passed away, but it was never funded with any assets. The estate-planning attorney didn't realize how important charitable giving was to my parents. Therefore, he did not understand the details of the assets enough to position them correctly. My mother was unable to ensure her lifestyle with a consistent stream of income, and there was no funding for the foundation or for any inheritance.

There are two "CEOs" in an affluent family. Typically, the one who made the money is the chief executive officer. The other CEO is the "chief emotional officer." Too often, the chief emotional officer is not part of the planning process. My father, the chief executive officer, failed in not involving my mother, the chief emotional officer, in his planning process. When the estate-planning attorney had questions, my mother was unable to provide the answers.

If you act now, then your wishes can be carried out accordingly. Your loved ones and those that you trust deserve to know your wishes and the expressions of your heart while you are still alive. What is the best investment of your resources to accomplish what you want done?

Your wealth plan should provide you with confidence about how you achieve your dreams and what the ultimate plans are for the use of your assets. You need a plan you can understand—one you are able to articulate for yourself, your family, and anyone else involved.

Leaving a Lasting Impression

Alexander the Great was one of the wealthiest rulers in the world. Before his death, he told his priests, "When you take me out for the funeral procession, make sure I'm sitting up, with my hand stretched out." He wanted to symbolize that even he, a great emperor, would leave this world with empty hands, with nothing. You cannot take your wealth with you. How do you want to be remembered when you're gone?

That is the planning that we really do. That's the significance we want to create in your life. It's a legacy of sorts. I was speaking at a medical conference in Washington, D.C., and at the end of my presentation, a gastroenterologist attending the conference approached me.

"You've probably never heard of me," he said, "but when I was in college, your father-in-law built housing for students like me who couldn't afford to pay for a dorm. I lived in your father-in-law's dorm, and he used to come in every morning at five o'clock to make sure that we were all awake and studying. I finished college because of your father-in-law."

When you give of yourself and you change the lives of others, you begin to create your significance. Furthermore, when you leave a legacy—be it a donation of money, a creation of a building, or a mark on someone's career—you leave a message for your children and your grandchildren, that this is the way they should live their lives.

I leave you with this note: Legacies can come in many forms, and one of the most important is the legacy of trust from one human to another—from friend to friend, from parent to child, or from client to advisor.

Afterword

To Advisors and Clients Alike: There's More to Life Than Chasing Commissions

I have been immensely blessed in these past fifty years in the United States. I've made a lot of money, and I've learned a lot. As an advisor, the most important thing I've learned is that there is a human being sitting on the other side of my desk who has phenomenal needs—and one of those is a need to be taken care of. When a client looks at you, the biggest thing on his mind is "Can I trust you?" So how, then, do you earn that trust? Not by pushing a product, but by understanding exactly what their needs are…and then understanding what their *wants* are.

If you ask clients about their biggest concerns, they'll tell you. Some clients frequently talk about fear, but we don't want to encourage that. What we want to tell them is that there are means of protecting themselves, that they don't have to panic, and that there is a huge abundance of tools to accomplish their goals.

Many high-net-worth clients go to CPAs and attorneys, and rely on them to cut taxes. As advisors, we need to understand that pain. As I learned from my strategic coach Dan Sullivan, there are two types of economies; the time and effort economy and the results-oriented economy. There is a shortage of well-trained CPAs in this country.

I empathize with my clients so much because I've both gone through and witnessed great pain. It was painful for me to see that so many people don't have opportunities, to see that there are people in the world who walk multiple miles a day to find clean drinking water. It hurt to see that there are some who cannot afford the bus fare to get to medical care, much less the medical care itself. This was the background that I came from, and as I've grown more successful over time, I've been able to not only empathize but also help.

You must be able to understand the background of your client. A friend of mine used to say, "Nobody cares how much you know until they know how much you care." It's all a matter of compassion and love and willingness to take on somebody else's problems.

I gravitate toward high-net-worth clients because, through them, I can help so many worthy charities and causes. The goal of one of my clients is to make sure that the children of incarcerated African-Americans don't end up in jail themselves. A staggering percent of those children do find themselves incarcerated at some point in their lives. My client's mission is to take care of those children. He loves, and he is gracious.

He's able to do this by working with me. We cut his taxes, set up his charitable trusts, and encouraged others to rally around his cause. There are needs everywhere, and you can make a difference and take that path from success to significance.

I was recently invited to give a speech in Fort Lauderdale, Florida, and my audience was comprised of forty very affluent Indian doctors. I ended my speech with information about my transition from success to significance. I told them that what I'm doing with my life now is no longer about taking care of myself but about making a difference, and that I got to that point by making sure I had a guaranteed paycheck for life. That gave me the freedom to do what I enjoy doing.

I continued on with some information about Sai Baba and building hospitals in India. At the end of my talk, a young couple from the audience approached me and told me they wanted to build a hospital in India, and I agreed to help them work out their finances so they could. I went to their house the next day to meet with them, and they told me, "We have twenty-two family members in this city, all doctors, and they're all interested in doing something like this. How can we help?"

You can make beautiful things happen if you're patient. You can make them happen if your goal is to make a difference and to help people. That's the journey I'm on that keeps me going at full speed. There are ways and means of helping yourself, but more importantly, you help yourself by helping others. You help yourself by making a difference. If you focus on the needs of those clients, they will take care of you. I had no idea that I would come across twenty-two doctors just because I was able to take care of one couple. This happens all the time, and my business grows, and my ability to help others grows.

I've learned to lead what I call a "four G life." The first G is for **gratitude**, and the final three are for **giving**: the power of giving, the power of giving back, and the power of giving forward. These four Gs are "high touch" concepts that can assist you in your transition from success to significance, whether you're an advisor or a client.

I wish you the best as you search for a life filled with joy and love. Remember the four Gs, and remember to find your significance. As you plan your finances, understand that money's worth is not simply cash value. You can use it as a tool for success. Take the steps to understand the meaning of money, and pave your future constructively.